Heliopolis: The History and Legacy of Ancient Egypt's Cult Center for the Sun God Atum

By Charles River Editors

David Schmid's picture of the Al-Masalla obelisk in Heliopolis

About Charles River Editors

Charles River Editors provides superior editing and original writing services across the digital publishing industry, with the expertise to create digital content for publishers across a vast range of subject matter. In addition to providing original digital content for third party publishers, we also republish civilization's greatest literary works, bringing them to new generations of readers via ebooks.

Introduction

A model of a votive temple gateway found at Heliopolis

Temple of the Aten in Amarna

Africa may have given rise to the first human beings, and Egypt probably gave rise to the first great civilizations, which continue to fascinate modern societies across the globe nearly 5,000 years later. From the Library and Lighthouse of Alexandria to the Great Pyramid at Giza, the Ancient Egyptians produced several wonders of the world, revolutionized architecture and construction, created some of the world’s first systems of mathematics and medicine, and established language and art that spread across the known world. With world-famous leaders like King Tut and Cleopatra, it’s no wonder that today’s world has so many Egyptologists.

What makes the accomplishments of the Ancient Egyptians all the more remarkable is that Egypt was historically a place of great political turbulence. Its position made it both valuable and vulnerable to tribes across the Mediterranean and the Middle East, and Ancient Egypt had no shortage of its own internecine warfare. Its most famous conquerors would come from Europe, with Alexander the Great laying the groundwork for the Hellenic Ptolemy line and the Romans extinguishing that line after defeating Cleopatra and driving her to suicide.

Perhaps the most intriguing aspect of ancient Egyptian civilization was its inception from the ground up, as the ancient Egyptians had no prior civilization which they could use as a template. In fact, ancient Egypt itself became a template for the civilizations that followed. The Greeks and the Romans were so impressed with Egyptian culture that they often attributed many attributes of their own culture–usually erroneously–to the Egyptians. With that said, some minor elements of ancient Egyptian culture were, indeed, passed on to later civilizations.

Egyptian statuary appears to have had an initial influence on the Greek version, and the ancient Egyptian language continued long after the pharaonic period in the form of the Coptic language.

Although the Egyptians may not have passed their civilization directly on to later peoples, the key elements that comprised Egyptian civilization, including their religion, early ideas of state, and art and architecture, can be seen in other pre-modern civilizations. Indeed, since Egyptian civilization represented some fundamental human concepts, a study of their culture can be useful when trying to understand many other pre-modern cultures.

Part of the reason Egyptian history is so intriguing is because it is so enigmatic – even today, despite the wealth of written materials and countless monuments, Egyptologists constantly uncover more mysteries about ancient Egypt, even if many of those mysteries are somewhat mundane and appeal more to academics. For example, historians still debate precise chronologies of dynasties, theological nuances, and architectural details.

The city of Heliopolis was one of ancient Egypt's most important religious centers, the focus of the civilization's solar cult, and a destination for pilgrims for nearly 3,000 years. It was at Heliopolis where Egyptian priests developed one of Egypt's three major creation myths, which, like any aspect of a culture that survived for as long as Egypt's did, evolved throughout the centuries. Heliopolis' origins were quite humble though, and it does not appear that it was ever planned to be a great city. The city began as a small settlement in the late 4th millennium BC, but within a couple of hundred years it became the center of Egypt's solar religion, due to several fortuitous circumstances.

Heliopolis' proximity to the political capital of Memphis no doubt helped with its early growth, as did its patronage by some important early kings. By the Middle Kingdom (c. 2055–1650 BCE), Heliopolis was one of the most important religious centers in Egypt, and the most important kings saw it as essential to erect monuments in the city. As Egypt's dynasties and kingdoms rose and fell, Heliopolis, the "City of the Sun," kept shining, attracting numerous kings to leave their mark. Throughout the New Kingdom (1550–1069 BCE) and the Late Period (728–332 BCE), Heliopolis continued to attract kings, sometimes foreigners, who wanted to establish their legitimacy as pharaohs.

Although Heliopolis faded and eventually disappeared as an important religious center after the Greeks and Romans took control of Egypt, its memory remained. The name Heliopolis is actually Greek for "city of the sun," while the Hebrews knew it as "On," proving that its historical memory was (and remains) quite strong.

Heliopolis: The History and Legacy of Ancient Egypt's Cult Center for the Sun God Atum examines the city and the various purposes it served. Along with pictures depicting important people, places, and events, you will learn about Heliopolis like never before.

Heliopolis' Origins

Although it's often forgotten now, the ancient Egyptians referred to Heliopolis in their own language as *Iunu*. The Greeks, who began visiting the city in the early 1st millennium BCE after it was already more than 2,000 years old, noticed that its importance was due to it being the center of the solar cult, so they began referring to it as the "city of the sun," or Heliopolis. Generally speaking, the Greeks viewed those outside of the Hellenic world as barbarians, but some of the older civilizations, such as Egypt, were worthy of their respect to a certain degree. The Greeks never learned the languages of these older, respected civilizations, so they applied their own names to many of the ancient cultures' cities and deities, and Egyptian deities were given Greek names according to the attributes they shared with their Greek counterparts. For instance, Ptah was known as Hephaestus because he was a metal worker, Amun was generally called Zeus, and Neith was referred to as Athena because both were female warrior deities. Atum and Re, the sun gods of Heliopolis, were called Helios.

All the while, the Egyptians continued to refer to the city as *Iunu* throughout their history. The name is derived from the Egyptian word *Iun*, which means "pillar." The spelling of Iunu in the Egyptian hieroglyphic script is a pillar with a "*nu*" pot and a determinative sign indicating a city (Faulkner 1999, 13). Long before the Greeks arrived in Egypt, the Hebrews had contact with the city and called it “On.”

Today, the city is located just to the northeast of modern Cairo, but little remains of its once former majesty. In ancient times, though, Heliopolis occupied a prime piece of real estate that no doubt contributed to its early growth. This is because ancient Heliopolis was located just north of Memphis on the southeast edge of the Nile Delta. Although the Egyptians mentioned *Iunu* in a number of different religious and historical texts, none of them explains why the city was built in its specific location. One theory is that Heliopolis formed and became a major center purely due to practical reasons, because Heliopolis is located along and near major east-west trade routes that connect Egypt to the Levant northeast of the Delta and Libya to the west (Nuzzolo and Krejčí 2017, 358).

Not long after the city grew in importance in the early Old Kingdom (c. 2686–2125 BCE), a canal was built that connected it to the Pelusiac branch of the Nile River, which integrated Heliopolis more along the traditional north-south axis of Egypt (Nuzzolo and Krejčí 2017, 360). There is little doubt that the canal made it much easier for pilgrims from other parts of Egypt to travel to Heliopolis since river barges were the primary mode of transportation in ancient Egypt, thereby helping the city grow. This canal linked to a vast canal network that connected Heliopolis to other nearby cities in the Delta that otherwise would have been separated from each other due to the course of the Nile and its branches. Thus, it seems certain that economics were taken into consideration when Heliopolis was built, at least initially.

Of course, since the city was primarily a religious center, a spiritual reason for its location must also be considered. In an age when science was rudimentary, the world was a vast, confusing, and often terrifying place of destruction, death and unexplained phenomena for the ancients. Not content with merely accepting their lot, early humans set about making sense of their existence by creating the teleological stories that later became the foundation of religion. By giving a phenomenon a story or its very own "history," the terrifying mystery could be somewhat tamed and play a part in the greater activity of understanding and participating in nature. Given this method, employed in service of early humans' tenacious pursuit of understanding, it is unsurprising that the earliest gods permeated every aspect of people's existences, and it is the interlacing web of these divine characters that makes those of the ancient Egyptians special.

According to the acclaimed Egyptologist Garry Shaw, the Egyptian ethos was "an endless repetition of creations, destructions and rebirths, entangled in a net of divine interactions … each person [living] as the hero of his own mythic narrative each day."[1] In this way, the ancient Egyptians would "assimilate" themselves with the corresponding deity that defined their situation at any given time. Shaw gives an enlightening set of examples on this topic, writing, "A person with a headache became Horus the Child, cared for by his mother, who herself became Isis; in death, the deceased transformed into various gods whilst traversing the afterlife realm, assuming each deity's divine authority for a time. Egypt's myths were elastic enough to be shaped into everyone's lives … myths, and the acts of the gods detailed therein, answered the question, 'why did this happen to me?' There is comfort in precedent."[2]

Relating oneself to "Horus the Child" would have been of especial importance for the ancient Egyptian, centered as it is within the concept of the ubiquitous "Divine Mother." One of the functions of the character of "divine mother" in world mythology is to maintain the sentiment of protectiveness and caregiving in early religions. Her role in the religious mindset of early humans was initially a dominant one, but in the 9th and 8th millennia BCE, when the androcentric nomadic cultures finally joined with the goddess-exalting societies that had built the first manifestations of the human desire for companionship and

---

[1] Shaw 2015

[2] Ibid.

protection, the more bellicose and "heroic" aspects of myth gained more religious prominence. To an ancient Egyptian, "becoming" Horus the Child was to find oneself in the protective embrace of the mother once more and to have the hope of convalescing and becoming stronger than before.

Horus's myth contributes to this religious mindset in two ways. On the one hand, Horus is the vanquishing hero of the divine royal line who epitomized "right" action and goodness over evil. On the other hand, he achieves that level of kingship only after being cared for as a sickly baby who was pursued by the evils of the world manifested by his uncle, Seth. This notion of assimilating oneself with Horus would have gone beyond mere semantic facility and would have given the believer a means of rationalizing the hostilities of the world around them. It also meant to inspire hope of finally vanquishing them and achieving adulthood and all the ambitions that came with it.

Every Egyptian was destined for eternity after death, but the Egyptians had no conception of an ethereal, otherworldly afterlife. Instead, the Egyptians believed that they would spend eternity in an eternal Egypt and that their lives there would mirror a perfect reflection of life as it had been lived in the Egypt of this earth. Eternal Egypt was known to ancient Egyptians by a few different names.

Most commonly, it was known as The Field of Reeds, but it was also commonly called Lily Lake and the Field of Plenty. Egyptian burial rites reflected this vision of eternity.

Scholars have established that the first Egyptian burial rites were practiced by 4000 BCE, and from that point until the Roman takeover of Egypt around 30 BCE, Egyptian burial rites demonstrated an unwavering focus on eternal life and the continuance of personal existence after death.[3]

Egyptian burial rites were very dramatic, even though Egyptians hoped that the deceased would find eternal bliss in the Field of Reeds. The ancient Greek historian Herodotus describes these dramatic rites: "As regards mourning and funerals, when a distinguished man dies, all the women of the household plaster their heads and faces with mud, then, leaving the body indoors, perambulate the town with the dead man's relatives, their dresses fastened with a girdle, and beat their bared breasts. The men too, for their part, follow the same procedure, wearing a girdle and beating themselves like the women. The ceremony over, they take the body to be mummified."[4]

---

[3] The ancient world was fascinated by the Egyptian burial, which became well known via cultural transmission through trade along the Silk Road. The Egyptian buran doubtless bore a great influenced on a number of other civilizations and religions—it was certainly a major source of inspiration for the Christian vision of eternal life.

[4] (Nardo, 110)

Mummification, by far the most well-known aspect of the Egyptian burial, was practiced in Egypt by the middle of the 3rd millennium BCE. Most scholars believe that mummification became common due to the way in which corpses were often preserved in Egypt's arid sands. At a very early point in the history of their civilizations, the Egyptians seem to have developed the concept of an eternal soul, and it was believed that the entire[5] body of the deceased needed to be preserved on Earth in order for that soul to be able to enjoy an eternal afterlife.

Once a person had died, his family would bring his body to the embalmers, where, as Herodotus explained, the professionals would "produce specimen models in wood, graded in quality. They ask which of the three [levels of service] is required, and the family of the dead, having agreed upon a price, leave the embalmers to their task…The best and most expensive model is said to represent [Osiris], the next best is somewhat inferior and cheaper while the third is cheapest of all."[6]

Even those Egyptians who couldn't afford to pay

---

[5] Ancient Egyptians believed that the soul consisted of nine separate parts. The physical body was known as the *Khat*; the *Ka* was one's double form; the *Ba* was a human headed bird aspect which was able to speed between earth and the heavens; *Shuyet* was the shadow self; *Akh* was the immortal, transformed self; *Sahu* and *Sechem* were aspects of the *Akh*; *Ab* was the heart, which was the source of good and evil; *Ren* was one's secret name. Without the *Ka* and the *Ba*, the *Khat* was believed to be unable to recognize itself.

[6] Ikram, 53; Nardo, 110. The three choices dictated not only what kind of coffin the deceased could be buried in, but also the funerary rites that would be available to him and the treatment of his body.

anything at all were given some kind of burial, as it was believed that the souls of the deceased who had not been properly buried would return as a ghost and spend eternity haunting the living.[7] The basic kind of mummification could be extremely expensive, so the poor often took to giving their used clothing to the embalmers so that it could be used to wrap the corpse.[8]

Once the corpse had been mummified, it was time for the funeral. The ancient Egyptians believed that the remembrance of the dead by the living ensured that the dead would continue to exist in the Field of Reeds. A great show of grief was thought to resound in the Hall of Truth (or Hall of Osiris)—the first major destination of

---

[7] The return of a ghost was considered to be a very serious matter, as the Egyptians were not able to tolerate the idea of non-existence. If the deceased was not given a proper burial (or if their loved ones had committed some sin before or after death), the gods gave the *Akh* dispensation to return to earth in order to redress the wrong. The Akh would then harass the living, who would have to plead their case to the ghost in the hopes of receiving a reasonable response. If they were not able to receive one themselves, a priest would have to intervene and serve as arbiter between the living and the dead. If, for example, misfortune were to befall a widower, that misfortune would first be attributed to some "sin" he had committed against his wife, who, omniscient in the Field of Reeds, was now punishing him. One such widower wrote a letter to his dead wife, begging her to leave him alone and insisting that he was innocent of any wrong-doing. The letter, which he delivered to her in her tomb, reads as follows: "What wicked thing have I done to you that I should have come to this evil pass? What have I done to you? But what you have done to me is to have laid hands on me although I had done nothing wicked to you. From the time I lived with you as your husband down to today, what have I done to you that I need hide? When you began to grow sick from the illness which you had, I caused a master-physician to be fetched…I spent eight months without eating and drinking like a man. I wept exceedingly together with my household in front of my street-quarter. I gave linen clothes to wrap you and left no benefit undone that had to be performed for you. And now, behold, I have spent three years alone without entering into a house, though it is not right that one like me should have to do it. This have I done for you sake. But, behold, you do not know good from bad." (Nardo, 32).

[8] Thus giving rise to the euphemistic phrase "the linen of yesterday" as a term for death which eventually came to be employed by the *Kites* (female professional mourners), who would lament that the deceased had once dressed in fine linens, but now slept in the linen of yesterday.

the deceased in the afterlife. Thus, the funeral was both an occasion to mourn the loss of the deceased and an occasion to celebrate and honor his life. Regardless of how popular the deceased may have been in life, it was traditional to have a group of professional mourners, called Kites, accompanying the funeral procession and burial. The Kites were paid to lament loudly throughout these proceedings, and traditionally, they would sing the "Lamentation of Isis and Nephthys," a lamentation song that had its origins in the myth of the two goddesses weeping over the death of Osiris. The song of the Kites was meant to inspire the other mourners at the funeral to show their emotion.

At some point prior to the funeral procession or immediately before placing the mummy in the tomb, a priest would perform the Opening of the Mouth Ceremony. This ceremony underscored the importance of the physical body; its purpose was to reanimate the corpse so that the immortal soul could continue to use it. In this ceremony, a priest recited spells while using a ritual blade to touch the mouth of the corpse—the touch of the blade was believed to enable the corpse to regain its ability to breathe, eat, and drink. Next, he touched the corpse's arms and legs so that it would be free to move about within the tomb (and beyond).

An ancient Egyptian mural depicting the opening the mouth ceremony

A mural depicting the opening the mouth ceremony for Tutankhamun

After the body was at last laid to rest, the tomb was sealed. Finally, the priest recited a number of other spells and prayers, usually the Litany of Osiris, and if the deceased was a pharaoh, the priest would recite a set of spells known as the Pyramid Texts. These were initially inscribed on the walls of the 5th Dynasty pyramid of Unas at Saqqara,[9] and they documented and gave advice to the king on his journey into the afterlife. These inscriptions

[9] Shaw 2015

were later copied onto other pyramids from the Old Kingdom and have therefore survived in good condition.

Unas Pyramid Text

In ancient Egyptian theology, the Benben stone also played a major role. It is believed that the original Benben stone located in Heliopolis may have been a meteorite, but whatever it was, it was believed by the Egyptians to be the primordial mound of creation (Wilkinson 2003, 99). The original stone is now lost, but several pictorial representations are still extant in ancient Egyptian art that depict it as a stone with a rounded top (Kemp 1991, 85). The original Benben stone provided the inspiration for the

Fifth Dynasty sun-temples in Abu Sir and was also probably an influence on the shape of pyramids, as well as the pyramidion on the top of New Kingdom obelisks (Kemp 1991, 88).

Jon Bodsworth's picture of the Benben stone from the Pyramid of Amenemhat III

The Fifth and Sixth Dynasty Pyramid Texts, which were hieroglyphic inscriptions on the inner chambers of kings' pyramids, describe the Benben stone as occupying a physical space in Heliopolis: "O Atum-Khoprer, you became high on the height, you rose up as the *bnbn*-stone in the Mansion of the 'Phoenix' in On, you expectorated

Tefenet, and you set your arms about them as the arms of a *ka*-symbol, that your essence might be in them." (Faulkner 2007, Utterance 600)

The Benben stone continued to be important throughout all phases of ancient Egyptian history, with one even existing in the city of Amarna during the reign of Akhenaten's (r. circa 1352–1336 BCE). This is significant because the city of Amarna was otherwise entirely dedicated to the worship of the Aten.

Although the physical Benben stone clearly played an important role in the history of Heliopolis specifically and more generally in ancient Egyptian religion, it is still unknown if it was the focal point of the actual solar cult in Heliopolis (Nuzzolo and Krejčí 2017, 366). The Benben stone may have been the focus of cultic and ritual functions of the priesthood at Heliopolis, or it may have been a more passive side piece that grew in symbolic and metaphysical importance even as its physical prominence waned.

Heliopolis' importance as one of Egypt's significant religious centers actually began before the Old Kingdom in the late Predynastic Period (c. 4000–3000 BCE). The Egyptian state had yet to be formed during this time, with local political centers exerting power over their respective regions, but the archaeological evidence from Heliopolis demonstrates that the Egyptians began their mortuary practice of preserving the dead during this period, as evidenced by 63 human graves (Nuzzolo and Krejčí 2017, 360). Although the graves are primitive by later Egyptian standards, the bodies, which were not mummified, were interred with simple household items such as pottery. Heliopolis was also the site of animal burials during the late Predynastic Period (Hornung 1996, 101), which was an early version of the animal necropolises that would become so common in ancient Egypt by the 1st millennium BCE. As with many ancient Egyptian necropolises, the Heliopolis necropolis attained a unique identity and a name: *Djet ahat net Iunu* ("The great eternity of Heliopolis") (Gelil et al. 1996, 139).

Legend has it that Menes, believed to be the first pharaoh of Egypt's First Dynasty, established his capital at Memphis by diverting the Nile River with dikes. Menes is also credited as being the first of Egypt's pharaohs to unite Egypt in a single, centralized monarchy. A 3rd century BCE Egyptian historian referred to this legendary pharaoh as Menes, but the 5th century Greek historian Herodotus gave his name as Min, and in the Ancient Egyptian native-king lists of the 19th dynasty, his name is listed as Meni.

Today, scholars have begun to speculate that the legendary pharaoh known as Menes was actually one of three archaic Egyptian pharaohs: Scorpian, Narmer, or Aha. Some have come to believe that the unification process took place over the reigns of several pharaohs and that Menes is simply a representation of all the pharaohs who were involved. According to Mantheo, however, the pharaoh Menes reigned for a full 62 years before he was at last carried off and killed by a hippopotamus.

Though the identification of Menes continues to prove difficult, it is clear that the first dynasty's rise to power was marked by an uptick in wealth. This is apparent from an increase in source materials such as inscriptions on stone vessels, ivory and wood labels, and seal impressions. These finds confirm that the first dynasty oversaw significant changes to the country's administration, namely the unprecedented expansion of the power of the central government. The available sources also testify to the construction of palaces and the founding of royal estates, as well as the naming of high-ranking government officials by which these processes were overseen.

Not surprisingly, the pharaohs of the first dynasty (~3000-2800 BCE) were fond of making demonstrations of their absolute power, but they did so in some unusual ways. During this period, it was apparently not uncommon for royal servants and some members of the royal elite to be killed or buried alive when the pharaoh's tomb was sealed, as they were expected to continue serving their ruler eternally in the afterlife.

Whoever Egypt's first pharaoh was, he established the political capital in the Lower Egyptian city of Memphis, and while it is unclear whether Heliopolis immediately benefited from its close proximity to Egypt's political capital, it is known that by the Second Dynasty, *Iunu* was the premier religious center in Egypt (Malek 2000, 92). The 3rd century BCE Hellenistic Egyptian priest and historian Manetho noted in his history of Egypt that by the Second Dynasty, Heliopolis was already the site of the cult of the sacred Mnevis Bull. Later historians transmitted the fragment as follows:

> "The Second Dynasty consists of nine kings of This. The first was Boêthos, for 38 years. In this reign a chasm opened at Bubastus, and many perished.
>
> "Kaiechôs, for 39 years. In his reign the bulls, Apis at Memphis and Mnevis at Heliopolis, and the Mendesian goat were worshipped as gods." (Manetho, *Aegyptiaca*. Fragment 8).

To date, there is still no direct evidence of building activity at Heliopolis in the First or Second Dynasties. It may be that archaeologists will uncover the remains of monuments from the Early Dynastic Period at Heliopolis, but for now the earliest archaeological evidence of building activity there is dated to the Third Dynasty.

The rulers of this dynasty greatly expanded their activity around Memphis. It is unclear where the first pharaoh of the dynasty, Sanakhte (2686-2668 BCE), was buried, but the second king of the dynasty, Djoser (2668-2649 BCE), chose Saqqara. Both rulers had active reigns, putting down rebellions and expanding their territory. It appears Djoser pushed as far south as Aswan and the First Cataract, which would be the southern border of Egypt for centuries to come, although some rulers moved even further south.

Saqqara was already established as a burial ground for Memphis, but Djoser and his architect Imhotep would turn it into something far grander. They decided to build the tomb in stone rather than mudbrick, and on a truly vast scale. There was nothing in previous Egyptian architecture that even came close to their achievement.

The origins of the pyramids, including their chosen shape and design, stretch all the way back to the mythological stories of the ancient Egyptians. As a culture, the Egyptians are known for their obsession with death, so it is ironic that these lavish tombs were inspired instead by a story of creation – the story of birth.[10] In

---

[10] Rosenberg, Donna. 1986. *World Mythology*. HARRAP, Great Britain. pp 166-177.

Egyptian mythology, the world was formed from out of the depths of a primal ocean that was both infinite and bereft of life, and these ancient waters parted when the sun rose for the very first time. This origin was something that the Egyptians referred to as the "first occasion". The chaotic waters of the lifeless ocean, an entity that they called Nu, parted as a pyramid shaped mound rose up through the waves. This shape, the benben, was the first part of Earth, the first sign of life, rising from out of the waters. The mythological imagery of Egypt naturally reflected the reality of their environment, where the rising waters of the Nile flooded the land, only to recede again and leave fertile ground with rich muds ready to be seeded with crops, the source of Egypt's bounty and life.[11]

While the shape of the pyramid derives from mythology, the Egyptians had several reasons for building them. The pyramids served religious and funerary purposes, while also serving as reinforcing power structures for Egypt's rulers, but the process of building also served a valuable practical function. Egypt required a large work force to produce the food needed to feed its people, as the rich soils surrounding the Nile needed to be seeded, crops tended and harvests reaped. For one entire season out of the year, however, the farming belt of Egypt was covered by water as the Nile flooded its banks, leading to a large

---

[11] Leeming, David Adams. 2010. *Creation Myths of the World.* AB.C.-CLIO, Santa Barbaro. pp 102.

part of Egypt's population being idle during that time. The building of monuments was a valuable method of keeping an otherwise idle population active, thereby guaranteeing employment for all throughout the year. Farmers in the Old Kingdom period who were idle and wanted to work during the Nile's period of inundation could get paid and avoid taxes by working on pyramid building projects. Egyptian citizens with nothing to occupy them while their farming lands were under water could thus spend the season erecting timeless monuments to their ruler, receiving wine and beer thrice daily as part of their working conditions.[12]

[12] Seawright, Caroline. 2013. *Egypt: The Nile Inundation*. Site accessed 4 September 2013. http://www.touregypt.net/featurestories/nile.htm

The Step Pyramid, also known as the Pyramid of Djoser

The Step Pyramid in Saqqara proved to be the final stepping stone in the creation of the true pyramid, but Imhotep was quite active throughout Egypt, and he more than likely helped his king leave his mark in Heliopolis. Archaeologists have been able to associate the oldest known structure in Heliopolis, a small shrine, with Djoser's reign (Malek 2000, 92). Due to his positions as lead royal architect and high priest, it is likely that Imhotep played a major role in the development of Heliopolis as a major religious center. In addition to the shrine that has been uncovered, Imhotep probably had more structures erected in the city, although at this point archaeologists have been unable to definitively identify any.

Since Imhotep was also a high priest, he also probably helped formalize the Heliopolitan priesthood. Egypt was essentially a theocratic state, so the priests wielded great power and influence. With that said, for most members of the priesthood their priestly duties were only a part-time position, because aside from the high priests, many priests were little more than local men who carried out more mundane duties around the temples (Shaw and Nicholson 1995, 228).

From an early point in the Old Kingdom, likely due to Imhotep's influence, the priesthood of Heliopolis became more organized and regimented. The high priest became known as the "Maa Wer," or "Great Seer," and later the "Wer Mau," or "Greatest of Seers," indicating that not only did the position have an esteemed place in Egyptian society, but that it is was also by then more than a mere part-time position (Shafer 1997, 9–10).

In fact, the early development of the Heliopolis priesthood was the most organized in the land, and one could argue the city's priesthood was the most elite of all Egyptian priesthoods for centuries. Due to the discipline and education of Heliopolis' priests, the city became known as a center of learning not only throughout Egypt, but also beyond the borders of the Nile Valley. When the Greek historian Herodotus visited Egypt in the 5th century BCE, he wrote that Heliopolis was known for being the educational backbone of Egypt: "There were other things, too, which I learnt at Memphis in conversation with the priests of Hephaestus, and I actually went to Thebes and Heliopolis for the express purpose of finding out if the priests in those cities would agree in what they told me with the priests at Memphis. It is at Heliopolis that the most learned of the Egyptians are to be found." (Herodotus, *The Histories*, Book II, 3).

Theology at Heliopolis

As the priesthood of Heliopolis grew in stature and reputation, its fundamental theology evolved with the political changes in Egypt.

From as early as the Early Dynastic Period, the country was divided into smaller dominions along the river that modern scholars call "Nomes". The word "nome" comes from the ancient Greeks who, during the rule of the Greek Ptolemaic dynasty (332-30 BCE) in Egypt, referred to each as a kind of "pasturage" coming under the overarching rule of the Pharaoh of that kingdom. This made for a useful way of organising the inhabitants of the two kingdoms, but it causes problems when trying to define what version of a common myth is the "correct" or "most widely believed". The reason for this is that the myths, though they had some similarities, could diverge widely from nome to nome. That is why writers such as the ancient historian Plutarch chose to single out a particular version of a myth and record or study it alone.

Later scholars further subdivided these various types of myth according to the cult center that either produced or "standardized" them.[13] They refer to them as "theologies," such as the "Memphite Theology" (myths from Memphis) or the "Heliopolitan Theology" (myths from Heliopolis).

---

[13] Shaw 2015

There is the theory that these "theologies" were competing in some way with others from different cult centers. Shaw, however, takes the view that they were more alternatives than opposing theories and although each cult center would substitute a god from another nome for one of their own local deities, there wasn't really any kind of animosity between the differing believers. Despite the fact that there was no externally enforced dogma over the whole of Egypt, the Egyptians still managed to maintain some overarching concepts. One such concept is that of the creation of the universe. Generally speaking, there was a limitless dark ocean of "chaos" called Nun, out of which a god was born who instigated creation.[14] The different cult centers felt at liberty to amend or augment that concept to incorporate local tastes and allegiances to deities. Later on, during the period of the New Kingdom, the cult center of Thebes gained prominence and the priests there tried to unify the earlier traditions of Egypt. In this attempt, Amun was the creator god but the Thebans also incorporated the traditions of the major cult centers like Hermopolis, Memphis and Heliopolis, which often seem quite disparate accounts to the modern reader but were quite ingeniously brought together at Thebes around 1200 BCE.[15]

The general creation story contains within it two aspects

[14] Shaw 2015
[15] Shaw 2015

that are crucial to understanding all of the myths of ancient Egypt: *maat* and *isfet*. Isfet represents chaos or disorder, generally speaking, and it was seen as a fundamental element of everything in existence. There was no notion of trying to eradicate isfet from their general lives in ancient Egypt; after all, it was said to be one of the elements that was present in the limitless ocean at the dawn of creation. The only desire for ancient Egyptians was that isfet never became more prevalent than maat, its opposite: justice. Maat was often depicted as a goddess wearing a feather on her head, which was also the hieroglyph that represented her.[16] She, or simply the concept of justice, was believed to be present in all aspects of life and if it was broken by anyone, there would be a punishment. According to the Middle Kingdom "Coffin Text" it was believed that Atum, the "Great Finisher" of creation,[17] inhaled maat in order to gain his consciousness: "Inhale your daughter Maat [said Nun to Atum] and raise her to your nostril so that your consciousness may live. May they not be far from you, your daughter Maat and your son Shu, whose name is "life" … it is your son Shu who will lift you up."[18]

After that, Atum was capable of making the waters of Nun recede away from him, making him rise above them

[16] Shaw 2015
[17] Shaw 2015
[18] 80 see Shaw 2015

and become "what remained" or the "mound of creation." It's important to take note of the fact that there was no creation until Atum inhaled life and justice. Therefore without maat and her dualistic counterpart, there would have been no world, and that is the reason for maat and isfet's ubiquity, as well as the acceptance of chaos in the world as seen by the ancient Egyptians. After Atum had separated himself from Nun, the children he kept inside, notably Shu and maat/isfet, often represented as a form of the goddess Tefnut, were now separated from their father, and Tefnut would go on to become the mother of all the gods.

Since each of the nomes had their own version of a given myth, collecting Egyptian myths into a definitive text was never possible. This has further exacerbated the mythologist's job, since these stories have survived in disparate versions and media.

The myths may have arrived at the hands of scholars from inscriptions on pyramid walls (such as the Old Kingdom's "Pyramid Texts"), painted on the inside of coffins (such as the Middle Kingdom's "Coffin Texts"), or texts written on papyri (such as the famous "Book of the Dead," which dates back to the Second Intermediate Period).[19] The mythologist's job is made even more exacting by the fact that, since the scribes who

---

[19] Shaw 2015

documented the myths assumed their readers were knowledgeable about the stories' details, they opted to refer to myths obliquely out of a sense of decorum. This was often the case for Osiris, whose death was a troublesome topic for those inscribing on the funerary monuments since it was thought that simply mentioning his death could "magically harm the deceased."[20]

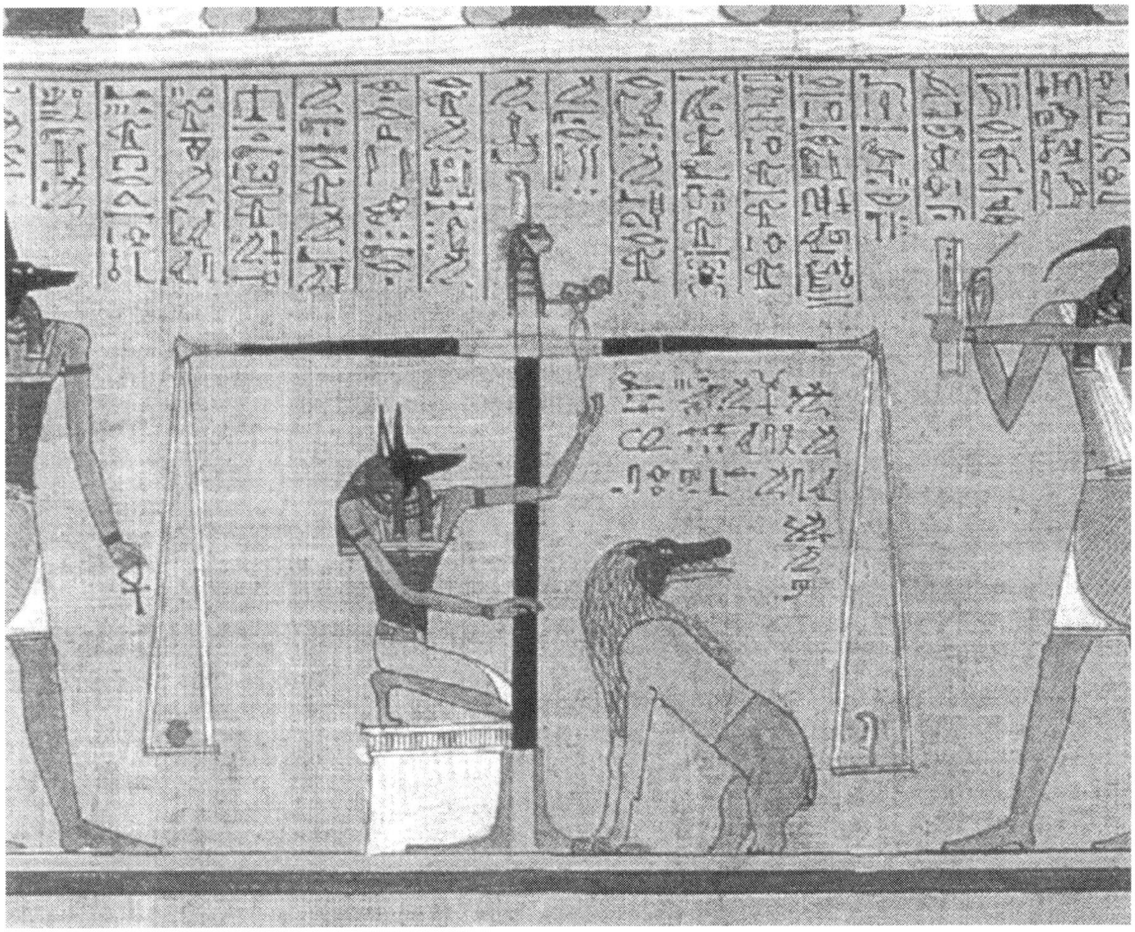

[20] Shaw 2015

Scenes from *The Book of the Dead*

As the name of the city indicates, Heliopolis began as the abode or cult center of the Egyptian solar and creator god Atum. During the first few dynasties of the Old Kingdom, Atum's preeminence was never in question, but the kings of the Fifth Dynasty (c. 2494–2345 BCE) began giving preference to another manifestation of the sun god, Re. The first king of the Fifth Dynasty, Userkaf (r. circa 2494–2487 BCE), built a temple specifically dedicated to Re at Abusir, just north of Saqqara, and although Heliopolis still retained its importance, Re became the primary solar god and was increasingly combined in a syncretic union with the older sun god as Atum-Re or Re-Atum (Nuzzolo and Krejčí 2017, 371).

Egypt entered the First Intermediate Period around 2160 BCE, which, as the name denotes, was a period of overall decline. The central government collapsed, and most major monument building ceased until Egypt was united once more by the Eleventh Dynasty, ushering in the

Middle Kingdom (c. 2055–1650 BCE). The Middle Kingdom rulers, especially those of the Twelfth Dynasty, expanded Egypt's borders south into Nubia and used those new resources to fund elaborate building programs.

The second king of the dynasty, Senusret I (r. circa 1956–1911 BCE), was particularly active at Heliopolis (Callender 2000, 161). There are both textual and archaeological sources that testify to Senusret I's building activities at Heliopolis, and Senusret I may have initiated the Heliopolitan building projects while he was coregent with his father, Amenemhat I (r. circa 1985–1956 BCE), in the third year of his rule (Redford 1992, 75). The centerpiece of the temple was an obelisk the king dedicated to Atum, which is still standing and is the only major monument at the site. It is also the oldest standing obelisk in Egypt (Grajetski 2009, 36).

The obelisk

The fact that Senusret I built at Heliopolis is both politically and religiously important. The Middle Kingdom originated in the southern Egyptian city of Thebes, and although the kings built in that city and patronized the city's primary god, Amun, as one of their favorites, they were politically astute enough not to forget the Delta and Lower Egypt. In time, the Twelfth Dynasty kings established a new royal capital near the modern town of Lisht in Middle Egypt, which signaled a compromise between Upper and Lower Egypt (Shaw and Nicholson 1995, 163). Senusret I's building activity at Heliopolis can also be interpreted as a move of political appeasement toward Lower Egypt just as much as it was religious patronage of the sun god.

Alone, the still standing obelisk Senusret I had constructed at Heliopolis may only be impressive due to its size, but when considered with an important historical text, it puts the importance and scope of the Atum Temple at Heliopolis into perspective. A New Kingdom hieratic text that served as a copy of a Middle Kingdom hieroglyphic inscription from the Atum Temple in Heliopolis described how the king ordered construction on the temple in his third year of rule: "Year 3, third month of inundation, day 8, under the Majesty of the King of upper and Lower Egypt, Kheperkare, the Son of Re, Sesostris, the justified, who lives forever and ever. . . Behold my majesty plans a work, thinks of a deed of value. For the future will I make a monument, I will settle form decrees of Harakhty. . . Having come as Horus, I have taken thought. Having established the offerings of the gods, I will construct a great house for my father Atum. He will enrich himself inasmuch as he made me conquer. I will supply his altars on earth. I will build my house in his neighborhood. My excellence will be remembered in his house: the shrine is my name, the lake my memorial. . . It is very good that you will make your monument in On, the sanctuary of the gods, near your father, the lord of the palace, Atum, the Bull of the Ennead. When your temple is built, it will provide for the altar. It will give service to your image. It will befriend your statues in all eternity." (Lichtheim 2006, 1:117). Harakhty is another version of Re, which coincides with the emergence of Re and the syncretic union of Re and Atum, although Senusret mentions Atum by name as well.

The archaeological evidence of Senusret I's activities and this important Egyptian text are further corroborated by an interesting Greek source that came far later. Greek historians and geographers such as Herodotus, Diodorus, and Strabo relished personality studies of various Egyptian kings, and though some of the details of those kings' lives were mistaken or possibly fabricated, one of the more interesting examples is the legend of "Sesoösis" related by the 1st century BCE Greek historian Diodorus in *Library of History*. Modern scholars believe that Sesoösis is actually a composite of several kings, namely the three Senusrets and Ramesses II (r. circa 1279–1213 BCE) (Krebsbach 2013, 101).

According to the legend, Sesoösis's incompetent son was aided by the oracle of Heliopolis, whom he repaid by dedicating two obelisks to the holy city. The historian wrote, “But his son, succeeding to the throne and assuming his father’s appellation, did not accomplish a single thing in war or otherwise worthy of mention, though he did have a singular experience. He lost his sight, either because he shared in his father’s bodily constitution or, as some fictitiously relate, because of his impiety towards the river, since once when caught in a storm upon it he had hurled a spear into the rushing current. Forced by this ill fortune to turn to the gods for aid, he strove over a long period to propitiate the deity by numerous sacrifices and honours, but received no consideration. But in the tenth year an oracular command was given to him to do honour to the god in Heliopolis and bathe his face in the urine of a woman who had never known any other man than her husband. Thereupon he began with his own wife and then made trial of many, but found not one that was chaste save a certain gardener’s wife, whom he married as soon as he was recovered. All the other women he burned alive in a certain village to which the Egyptians because of this incident gave the name Holy Field; and to the god in Heliopolis, out of gratitude for his benefaction, he dedicated, in accordance with the injunction of the oracle, two monolithic obelisks, eight cubits wide and one hundred high.” (Diodorus, *Library of History*, I, 59).

After getting beyond the bizarre and unbelievable part

about the king burning several women alive, the final statement about the erection of the obelisks seems truthful and corroborates the Berlin Leather Role and the extant obelisk at Heliopolis from Senusret I's reign. The fantastic story also corresponds to the historical fact that Senusret I's son and successor, Amenemhat II (r. circa 1901–1867 BCE), is also known to have built at Heliopolis.

While there is no reason to believe that Amenemhat II did anything remotely close to what Diodorus suggested in the Sesoösis legend, the archaeological and written evidence indicates that he was far below his father's mark in terms of influence. With that said, there is evidence that the king did take an interest in Heliopolis as the legend states, and there are a few statues associated with Amenemhat II that were discovered in various places throughout Egypt that mention the city. One particularly interesting statue is a colossal sphinx discovered in the Third Intermediate capital city of Tanis but has been assigned Heliopolis as a provenance due to its accompanying inscription (Grajetski 2009, 47). Thus, even if Amenemhat II's building activities in Heliopolis have (at least so far) been revealed to be not so impressive, they were substantial enough to have possibly influenced the Sesoösis legend.

Heliopolis also played a peripheral role in the historical memory of another non-Egyptian people. The history of the Hebrews has often been a source of controversy because the Old Testament is the only historical source that offers details, and while archaeology and the written sources of non-Hebrew peoples such as the Egyptians have helped develop a general outline of history before the Kingdom of Israel, debate still rages over the Hebrews' sojourn in Egypt and their subsequent Exodus. Historians still argue over the historicity of Genesis and Exodus, but it is worth pointing out that Heliopolis was mentioned in a few passages.

Heliopolis is mentioned in reference to Joseph's work with the pharaoh, and according to Egyptologists and Biblical scholars who believe the historicity of the Hebrew sojourn in Egypt, the patriarch Abraham entered Egypt sometime in the Tenth Dynasty, or the First Intermediate Period (Redford, 258–59). This would mean that Joseph served one of the early Middle Kingdom pharaohs.

The book of Genesis states that Joseph was given a Heliopolitan priest's daughter in marriage: "And Pharaoh called Joseph's name Zaph-nath-paaneah; and he gave him to wife Asenath the daughter of Poti-pherah priest of On. And Joseph went out over all the land of Egypt." (Gen. 41:45). Since Joseph was also made the king's primary advisor (Gen. 41:46), his arranged marriage to the high priest of Heliopolis' daughter validates the importance of the Heliopolitan priesthood, as discussed earlier.

The priest of Heliopolis was truly powerful politically, but the theology they espoused had an even more profound impact on pharaonic history. One of the curious features of ancient Egyptian religion and mythology is that there was not just one, but three primary creation myths, each associated with a major city, but the three myths could exist simultaneously in the minds of the Egyptians.

The three cosmogonies essentially represented three different ways in which anything can be created. The Hermopolitan creation was one in which creation was latent and waiting to happen, while the Memphite took place through thought and expression. The Heliopolitan cosmogony was perhaps the most tangible and concrete of all the ancient Egyptian cosmogonies. Creation took place through the sun, and it was the sun that gives life to everything (Wilkinson 2003, 17–19).

According to the Heliopolitan creation myth, all life arose from a primordial mound. The sun god Atum was the first sentient being to come from the mound, which happened purely through his own will (the name Atum is derived from the Egyptian word *tem*, meaning “complete” or “total”) (Wilkinson 2003, 99; Faulkner 1999, 298).

Once Atum created himself, he set about to create the first four pairs of deities – known as the "Ennead" – monosexually.

The so-called "Utterances" or verses from the Pyramid Texts of the Fifth and Sixth Dynasties relate some of the details of this creation. In one Utterance, it states Atum gave life through his spit: "Stand upon it, this earth which issued from Atum, this spittle which issued from Khoprer; come into being upon it, be exalted upon it, so that your father may see you, so that Re may see you." (Faulkner 2007, Utterance 222).

Another Utterance claims that the creation of the Ennead happened when Atum masturbated: "Atum is he who (once) came into being, who masturbated in On. He took his phallus in his grasp that he might create orgasm by means of it, and so were born the twins Shu and Tefenet. May they put the King between them and set the King among the gods in front of the Field of offerings." (Faulkner 2007, Utterance 527)

Although the examples may seem to contradict each other, since the Egyptians believed that three different creation myths could coexist simultaneously, so too could different versions exist simultaneously of the same myth. The importance of the Heliopolitan cosmogony is not so much in the details, but the general ideas that Atum was created through self-will and that he created the next generation of gods from his own body.

The Ennead consisted of Atum and his eight direct descendants, the first two pairs of which were elemental in nature. Shu (air) was the first male deity created after Atum, with his consort Tefnut (moisture). The next pair created was Geb (earth) and his divine wife Nut (sky). The final two pairs were then created simultaneously, representing the transition from divinity to the temporal world: Osiris and Isis and Seth and Nephthys (Wilkinson 2003, 79). The deities of the Ennead were mentioned frequently in the Pyramid Texts, but often separately in their various functions that assisted the deceased king in his journey through the afterlife. In one Utterance they are all mentioned together as a unit riding a solar barge through the night sky, assisting the dead king on his journey:

> "My father ascends to the sky among the gods who are in the sky; he stands at the Great Polar Region and learns the speech of the sun-folk.
>
> "Re finds you on the banks of the sky as a waterway-traveller who is in the sky: 'Welcome, O you who have arrived', say the gods. He sets his hand on you at the zenith of the sky; 'Welcome, O you who know your place', say the

Ennead.

> "Be pure; occupy your seat in the Bark of Re, row over the sky and mount up to the distant ones; row with the Imperishable Stars, navigate with the Unwearying Stars, receive the freight of the Night-bark.
>
> "May you become a spirit which is in the Netherworld, may you live of that pleasant life whereof the Lord of the Horizon lives, (even) the Great Flood which is in the sky. 'Who has done this for you?' Say the gods who serve Atum." (Faulkner 2007, Utterance 513).

Atum and Re are mentioned separately in the Utterance but are virtually indistinguishable in terms of their function as the solar god.

The Heliopolitan creation myth was essentially complete when it was first inscribed on the pyramid interiors during the Fifth Dynasty, and the city of Heliopolis and the Heliopolitan myth continued to play an important role in Egyptian society (Tobin 2002, 240). Little was added to the idea of the Atum and his creation of the Ennead, but a mythic cycle about the final two pairs of the Ennead became popular in the New Kingdom, and the Greeks even recorded their own version of the Heliopolitan myth, albeit in a way that confused it with other Egyptian cosmogonies as well as Greek myth. Diodorus wrote, "And besides these there are other gods, they say, who were terrestrial, having once been mortals, but who, by reason of their sagacity and the good services which they rendered to all men, attained immortality, some of them having even been kings in Egypt. Their names, when translated, are in some cases the same as those of the celestial gods, while others have a distinct appellation, such as Helius, Cronus, and Rhea, and also the Zeus who is called Ammon by some, and besides these Hera and Hephaestus, also Hestia, and, finally, Hermes. Helius was the first king of the Egyptians, his name being the same as that of the heavenly star." (Diodorus, *Library of History*, I, 59). Helius is Atum, or Atum-Re, while Hephaestus was Ptah and Hermes was Thoth, which demonstrates that the Heliopolitan myth had a profound influence that lasted for centuries after the Fifth Dynasty and even extended beyond Egypt's borders.

The creation myth that was first formulated in Heliopolis was also representative of some of ancient Egypt's most important general theological and political concepts. Among the three major Egyptian cosmogonies, the Heliopolitan myth had the most profound influence on the solar theology, and the solar theology proved to be among the most important aspect of Egyptian theology throughout all periods of history and in many ways defined the ancient Egyptians as a people. Solar imagery was apparent in royal names (the "Son of Re" name) and art, as well as in religion and myth. The sun god was responsible for giving life to the people and the land, as the sun was needed to make the crops grow to protect the land from the forces of darkness. The sun god was also responsible for giving life after death. According to the Pyramid Texts, the different manifestations of the sun god helped the dead king ascend from his earthly body and reach the domain of the gods.

Although Re began replacing Atum as the more important manifestation of the sun god by the Fifth Dynasty, both were seen as essential in the resurrection of the king in the Heliopolitan theology (Wilkinson 2003, 79). Re eclipsed Atum in importance in later periods, even at Heliopolis (Wilkinson 2003, 101), but the concept that the two represented different sides of the same solar theology began in the Old Kingdom. As the priests of Heliopolis developed the cosmology of Heliopolis during Egypt's first five dynasties, Re began to be seen as the rising sun and Atum as the setting sun (Wilkinson 2003, 100). The syncretism of Atum and Re was referenced in numerous Utterances of the Pyramid Texts, especially with regards to resurrection and life after death.

One notable Utterance combines the solar gods as they help the deceased king travel through the afterlife: "O Re-

Atum, this King comes to you, an imperishable spirit, lord of the affairs(?) of the place of the four pillars; your son comes to you, this King comes to you. May you traverse the sky, being united in the darkness; may you rise in the horizon, in the place where it is well with you. . . O Osiris and Isis, go and proclaim to the gods of Lower Egypt and their spirits: 'This King comes indeed, an imperishable spirit, as one to be worshipped, who is in charge of the Nile. Worship him, you spirits who are in the waters! Whom he wishes to live will live; whom he wishes to die will die.'" (Faulkner 2007, Utterance 217).

Osiris and the other final generation of the Heliopolitan Ennead would continue to play an important role in Egyptian religion well into the Roman occupation, and the well-developed mortuary rituals of the New Kingdom and Late Period can trace their origins directly back to Heliopolis and the role that the Ennead played in Egyptian religion.

Heliopolis was also instrumental in royal Egyptian ideology and other more esoteric ideas about the nature of life and time. Royal ideology was central to most elements of ancient Egyptian religious and political thought - since the Egyptians believed that their kings were gods, the Egyptian state was a theocracy ruled by a divine being. The origin of this philosophy can be traced back to Heliopolis and the Ennead, with Osiris being the first temporal king. Although Osiris was later murdered by his brother Seth, the gods gave the throne to Horus and every subsequent king was seen as the living incarnation of that god (Wilkinson 2003, 79). Atum was also directly associated with kingship in texts and in iconography. In artistic renderings he was usually depicted in human form wearing the double crown of Upper and Lower Egypt (Tobin 2002, 246).

Finally, Heliopolis also influenced Egyptian theology in less apparent, more esoteric ways. The Egyptians had no problem believing in more than one creation myth simultaneously, and the same applied to time. Egyptians believed that time was fundamentally cyclical and that there is a period of preexistence, a primeval period, and historical time, which can clearly be traced back to Heliopolis and its cosmogony (Assman 2001, 121). In other words, the periods of time related in the Heliopolitan myth had happened before, were taking place in the present, and would happen again at some point in the future.

Heliopolis in the New Kingdom

Egypt during the New Kingdom reached the height of its power, wealth, and influence. At the height of the New Kingdom, Egypt controlled Nubia all the way down to the fourth cataract and the Levant as far north as Ugarit. Gold and electrum entered Egypt from the south, and timber, horses, and precious stones came from the east and north, with much of it eventually ending up in the temples. Although Amun, the primary god of Thebes, rose in prominence during the New Kingdom, Atum-Re and Heliopolis also rode the waves of imperial Egypt's might. The kings of the Eighteenth, Nineteenth, and early Twentieth Dynasties used the booty from the numerous military campaigns and the lucrative colonies they established to aggrandize Heliopolis as had never been done before, and since the New Kingdom was a period of increased literacy as well as wealth, there are far more extant written records that detail the building activity in *Iunu*.

The Second Intermediate Period (c. 1650–1550 BCE), like the First Intermediate Period, was a time when the central government in Egypt failed, but instead of competing native Egyptian dynasties fighting for power, the Second Intermediate Period was marked by a foreign group known as the Hyksos coming to power in the Nile Delta. Heliopolis fell under the control of the Hyksos as well, but there is little evidence of the Hyksos presence in Iunu.

That said, it is known that the first king of the Eighteenth Dynasty and the New Kingdom, Ahmose I (r. circa 1550–1525 BCE), entered Heliopolis on his way north in the protracted military campaign that drove the Hyksos from Egypt (Redford 1992, 128). Once the Hyksos were expelled from the Delta, the early Eighteenth Dynasty kings dedicated much of their religious and political activities to the Thebes region, although Memphis once more became a political capital and Heliopolis recaptured its place as the center of the solar religion.

The expansion of Egypt's borders during the New Kingdom was accomplished by several kings in the early Eighteenth Dynasty, but none more than Thutmose III (r. circa 1479–1425 BCE). The warrior king personally led campaigns into the Levant, and by the end of his rule the Egyptian army had campaigned dozens of times in the Levant and Nubia, pushing the imperial boundaries to their greatest extent.

Thutmose III dedicated plenty of resources to the temple complex of Karnak in Thebes, but according to inscriptions from that and other places, he also gave numerous offerings to Heliopolis and built in the holy city (Bryan 2000, 244). Part of the inscription reads, "_______ yearly; consisting of loaves, bull-calves, bulls, fowl, incense, wine, fruit, every good thing of the dues of each year. My majesty established divine offerings, in order to gain the favor of (my) father, Harakhte, when he rises ______ my majesty [established for] him a divine offering of barley, in order to perform the ceremonies therewith, at the feast of the new moon, at the feast of the sixth day (of the month); and as a daily (income) of each day, according to that which was done in Heliopolis. Behold, my majesty found it very good to plow the barley in ______" (Breasted 2001: 2:224).

There is also archaeological evidence of Thutmose III's building activity that is now located in London. When the ancient Greeks and Romans visited and ruled over Egypt, they were impressed with the country's many monuments. The Greeks considered the Pyramids of Giza one of the Seven Wonders of the World, and the Romans began the long tradition of taking ancient Egyptian antiquities and transporting them to Europe. The Romans were particularly fascinated with obelisks, many of which were 70 feet or taller and made from single granite blocks. Roman emperors took obelisks from Egypt to Rome, and at least one was taken from Heliopolis to Alexandria before the British brought it to London in the 19th century (Breasted 2001, 2:254).

The inscription on the London obelisk indicates that it was one of a pair Thutmose III had built in Heliopolis: "Thutmose (III); he made (it) as his monument for his father, Harakhte, erecting for him two great obelisks; with pyramidion of electrum, at the fourth occurrence of the jubilee, because he so loved [his father.] May the Son of Re, Thutmose (III), be [given life] through him."

(Breasted 2002, 2:254).

Ethan Doyle White's picture of the obelisk in London

The text helps present a clearer picture of what Heliopolis must have looked like during the New Kingdom. In addition to the obelisks built there during Senusret I's rule, the obelisks dedicated by Thutmose III would have given the temple a look similar to those in Memphis and Thebes. It more than likely followed a similar layout as the New Kingdom temples in Karnak, Thebes, and Medinet Habu, and the city would also have been similar in size.

The importance of Heliopolis never diminished, despite being overshadowed by the Hyksos occupation, and the kings of the Eighteenth Dynasty appear to have been eager to put the holy city back in its proper place. Thutmose III's successor, Amenhotep II (r. circa 1427–1400 BCE), followed the pattern of conducting military campaigns into the Levant and Nubia for resources. Also like his predecessor, he used the booty to add to existing temples and leave inscriptions that memorialized his work.

One particularly interesting inscription, left at the Elephantine/Abu temple in Upper Egypt, relates how the king was victorious in the northern Levant (Upper Retenu). Although the temple was far from Heliopolis and dedicated primarily to the god Khnum, Amenhotep II referred to himself as the "Ruler of Heliopolis." The inscription reads, "Then his majesty caused that this tablet should be made and set up in this temple in the place of the Station of the King, and engraved with the great name of the Lord of the Two Lands, the Son of Re, Amenhotep (II), Divine Ruler of Heliopolis in the house of the fathers, the gods, after the return of his majesty from Retenu the Upper, having overthrown all his enemies, extending the boundaries of Egypt, on the first victorious campaign." (Breasted 2001: 2:312).

The influence of Heliopolis and the Eighteenth Dynasty kings' association with the city and temple continued with the reigns of Thutmose IV (r. circa 1400–1390 BCE) and Amenhotep III (r. circa 1390–1352 BCE). Thutmose IV is known to have erected monuments at Heliopolis and favored the sun god and the Heliopolitan theology. The primary inscription that details Thutmose IV's interest in the Heliopolitan solar theology is from the Sphinx in front of the Great Pyramids of Giza. According to a stela erected near the Sphinx by Thutmose IV, he cleared sand away from the monument to honor the gods, especially Atum-Re-Horakhti of Heliopolis (Bryan 2000, 255). Part of the stela reads, "Live the Good God, son of Atum, Protector of Harakhte, living image of the All-Lord; sovereign, begotten of Re; excellent heir Khepri; beautiful of face like his father; who came forth [_] equipped with the form of Horus upon him, a king who – the gods; who – favor with the Ennead of gods; who purifies Heliopolis, who satisfies Re." (Breasted 2001, 2:322).

The above text demonstrates two important points relating to Heliopolis and its theology. The first important point is that the city and its theology continued to hold sway over the kings of the New Kingdom. Although Amun, the god of Thebes, was rising in popularity (as was the Hermopolitan theology), Atum and Heliopolis still played a central role in Egyptian religion. Moreover, the details of the sun god were also still evolving by the Eighteenth Dynasty, and the syncretic union that began taking place between Atum and Re in the Fifth Dynasty had continued and involved other solar deities by the Eighteenth Dynasty, including Horakhti and the beetle-god Khepri.

The prominence of the solar theology reached its apex during Amenhotep III's reign. Although he was known for primarily building around Thebes, he is also credited with monuments at Heliopolis and other eastern Delta sites (Bryan 2000, 265). The iconography of Amenhotep III's artwork was associated with the solar theology much more than previous kings, although its incarnation usually cited was Re and eventually the sun-disk, Aten (Shaw and Nicholson 1995, 29).

A statue of Amenhotep III

The solar cult had been an important part of Egyptian religion since the Old Kingdom, but Amenhotep III took things much further. Not only did he seemingly worship different manifestations of the sun god above all others, he seemingly only worshipped the sun god. The emphasis on the solar cult was then followed by Amenhotep III's son and successor, Akhenaten (r. circa 1352–1336 BCE).

A depiction of Akhenaten, Nefertiti, and their children

By his fifth year of rule, Akhenaten apparently determined that the Aten could not shine as it needed to in the shadow of Egypt's older gods, so he decided to move north and build a new city dedicated completely to the Aten, like he was. The death of Amunhotep III may have also played a role in the king moving his operations away from Thebes, but either way, the stage was set for the king to change his name and the way in which gods would be viewed in the Nile Valley.

Amarna was a city that was purposefully built for its ruler to focus attention on the worship of the god Aten, so it was not a city that grew and developed over time, but it must have been nothing short of remarkable. During what is today termed the Amarna Period, much of what is known about life at that time comes from three main sources. The first source is art, including stelae, non-royal tombs, royal tombs, sculptures, etc. The second source is a set of documents, known as the Amarna tablets, and the third source is archaeological data.

Much of the art was found in the tombs near the city, which contained the remains of Akhetaten's elite inhabitants. The art includes multiple depictions of life in Akhetaten, like scenes of the king racing chariots from the North royal palace down to the southern administration palace. Other scenes depict the king rewarding and appointing his officials, not from a throne room but from a balcony of the Southern palace. In other depictions the temple of Aten is a feature. Small shrines from private homes could be found with images of the royal family, including one that shows the king and queen playing with their young daughters.

Once the construction of the city was completed, Akhenaten had two boundary stelae erected to mark the limits of the city, one in the north and one in the south. A boundary stela is an inscription on a stone block, generally called a "stela" (plural stelae), which relates the limits of either a kingdom or in this case a city. Boundary stelae always stated what king had the monument erected, what year it was built, and often some details such as why the boundary was established. The southern stela was later replaced, and today only about a third of the replacement is extant (Murnane 1995, 73).

The text is significant because it explicitly stated that the city would be the new cult center of the Aten: "Since he casts them on me, in life and dominion continually forever, I shall make Akhet- Aten for the Aten, my father, in this place. I shall not make Akhet-Aten for him south of it, north of it, west of it (or) east of it. I shall not go past the southern stela of Akhet-Aten toward the south, nor shall I go past the northern stela of Akhet -Aten downstream, in order to make Akhet-Aten for him there. Nor shall I make <it> for him on the western side of Akhet-Aten; but I shall make Akhet-Aten for the Aten, my father, on the orient (side) of Akhet-Aten – the place which he himself made to be enclosed for him by the mountain, on which he may achieve happiness and on which I shall offer to him. This is it!" (Murnane 1995, 76-77).

Akhenaten also made it very clear that he is the only one with the answer when it comes to building the new city and worshipping the Aten: "Nor shall the King's Chief Wife say to me, 'Look, there's a nice place for Akhet-Aten someplace else,' nor shall I listen to her. Nor shall any officials in my presence – be they officials of favor or officials of the outside, or the chamberlains, or any people in the entire land – say to me, 'Look, there's a nice place for Akhet-Aten someplace else,' nor shall I listen to them – whether it (=that other place) be downstream, whether it be in the south, in the west or in the orient. I will not say, 'I shall abandon Akhet-Aten so that I may hasten and make Akhet-Aten in this other nice place [. . .] together with it forever': but [I will remain] in this Akhet-Aten, with which he himself has wished to be satisfied forever and ever." (Murnane 1995, 77).

Akhenaten truly had all the control in the new capital, from what god was worshipped to the layout of the city. Due to the passage of time, most ancient Egyptian cities are now far below modern cities and will never be completely uncovered, but since Amarna is such a small village and was built just outside the site of ancient Akhet-Aten, the complete structure of the city has been accurately blueprinted by modern scholars. The city was built along a north-south axis that roughly followed the river, and the primary cluster of economic and religious activity would have taken place in what modern scholars refer to as the Central City. As the name indicates, the Central City was located geographically in the center of Akhet-Aten, but it was also in the spiritual center of the capital. Both the Great and Small Aten temples were located in the Central City along with one of the king's homes. Other important government offices were also located in the Central City, including the record's office, a military post, and the city's primary bakery, making it a central business district. Thus, the Central City would have been the hub of activity and full of people on any given day, and priests, peasants, soldiers, and nobles all would have rubbed shoulders as they conducted their daily affairs in the Central City. A north-south "royal road" connected the central area to the housing and tombs north and south (Kemp 1991, 271).

Limestone reliefs depicting Akhenaten, Nefertiti and three of their daughters with the Aten represented as beams of light

Although Akhenaten dedicated his worship and patronage to the disk of the sun, the Aten, even in building the new city of Amarna for the god, he followed in the solar theology tradition that began in Heliopolis. Akhenaten was also obviously aware of the connection that the Aten had with Heliopolis, no matter how far removed, as the king had an Aten temple built in Heliopolis (Dijk 2000, 286). There is also evidence that he continued to care for the sacred Mnevis bull in Heliopolis. The Mnevis bull was an especially important aspect, not just of Heliopolis, but of Egypt generally. The bull was believed to be the living incarnation of the sun god, and there was only one living at a time. The all black bull was cared for by the priests of Heliopolis and when he died, he was mummified and given a burial fit for a king (Shaw and Nicholson 1995, 189).

The 1st century BCE Greek geographer Strabo wrote about the Mnevis bull in his description of Egypt: “Here are both the city Bubastus and the Bubastite Nome; and above it is the Heliopolite Nome. In this Nome is Heliupolis, which is situated upon a noteworthy mound; it contains the temple of Helios, and the ox Mneuïs, which is kept in a kind of sanctuary and is regarded among the inhabitants as god, as is Apis in Memphis. In front of the mound are lakes, which receive the overflow from the neighboring canal.” (Strabo *Geography*, XVII, I, 27).

A votive stela depicting the Mnevis bull

After Akhenaten's rule, Egypt entered into a period that is today chronologically confusing and not fully understood. It is believed that Tutankhamun ascended to the Egyptian throne in 1336 BCE, and at that time his royal praenomen was Tutankhaten, not Tutankhamun. He would have only been a child of around 9 years of age when he became Egypt's ruler, but he was not the first child of the Eighteenth Dynasty to ascend the throne, as both Thutmose III and Amenhotep III ascended the throne at very young ages as well. Unlike Tutankhamun, however, those earlier kings had female regents to help rule on their behalf until they came of age. Hatshepsut famously ruled not only as regent but as the king in her own right on behalf of her stepson Thutmose III, while Mutemwiya was Amenhotep III's regent.

None of this may ever be known with certainty, but what is known is that the 9-year-old Tutankhamun came to the throne without a female regent. The position of trusted advisor was taken by another, one who was not even of the royal family. This replacement for the position of regent was taken by a man called Horemheb who bore no familial ties to Tutankhamun but was the senior commander of the army. How he came to be the commander of the Egyptian army is well documented in his own "Coronation text", which is inscribed on the back of a statue now in the Turin Museum, but why he was chosen to be Tutankhamun's advisor is not clear.

Given the young king's age, it should come as no surprise that Horemheb became the strong arm behind the throne, and he was even granted titles that implied he would have had the right to claim the throne in the event of Tutankhamun died without bearing any royal offspring. With the support of the military, Horemheb was able to quickly initiate strong policy changes in Egypt.

Within the first year of his reign Tutankhamun's name was changed from Tutankhaten to Tutankhamun, which means "ruler of southern Heliopolis". This was a direct and pointed reference to Karnak and the cult of the sun god Amun-Ra. Tutankhamun's name was not the only thing that changed. The royal court quickly abandoned Akhetaten and moved to Memphis, and although the city continued to be occupied for a time, it quickly fell into disuse and ruin. It's clear Horemheb was quickly seeing to the re-establishment of the "old ways".

Tutankhamun's reign is often referred to as the "Restoration," an apt name for his rule, or more accurately, for Horemheb's policies. The Restoration Stele is arguably the most important document of Tutankhamun's reign, as it details the so-called chaos that was brought about by Akhenaten's policies. According to the document, the gods had abandoned Egypt and the Egyptians, prayers were no longer listened to, the once great military met continued defeat in the east, and they were unable to defend their ally the Mitanni, they were losing territories throughout their northern frontier. Egypt had lost its way, particularly in the eyes of the military, and Horemheb now saw his chance to change all this with Tutankhamun's ascension to the throne. Early on in Tutankhamun's reign the traditional cults in Egypt were re-established, the military began further campaigns in the east fighting the Hittites, and Egypt's control over Nubia was expanded. Horemheb oversaw the militaristic expansion of the kingdom, while the chief treasurer Maya, oversaw the administrative re-organization and restoration of the cults. Maya also became responsible for the demolition of the temples and images of Aten, first focusing on those in Thebes and then on Amarna itself. It was this act of demolition that left Amarna bare, and led to its final abandonment. It is believed that Maya may have also been responsible for the removal of Akhenaten's mummy from his tomb in Amarna to a small tomb in the Valley of the Kings, KV 55, at least if the body found in KV 55 was indeed that of Akhenaten.

Statue of Akhenaten in the early Amarna style

Even though Tutankhamun and his advisors made a decided effort to restore Egypt's religious traditions, 20 years of the traditional cults being suppressed and the promotion of the sun god Aten had left its mark on Egypt's people. The political and cultural changes that took place during Tutankhamun's reign can be most easily understood by a study of the funerary changes that occurred. Such changes may be tracked through the developments found in tomb architecture that occurred during Tutankhamun's reign, and they endured throughout the rest of the New Kingdom Period. In Thebes the rock cut tombs of the past continued to be the norm, but there were changes made to their architecture and decoration. They were adapted to portray the new views of a tomb being a private mortuary temple for its owner, and the funerary cult became integrated with the cult of Osiris, who was now viewed as being the nocturnal manifestation of Ra. Solar symbolism had become increasingly popular during the reign of Amenhotep III, and it was made paramount during the Amarna period with the sole worship of the sun god Aten. Under Amenhotep III, Ra-Horakty was the primary sun deity, symbolized by a falcon headed man, while during the Amarna period under Akhenaten, the Aten was depicted is a sun disk, with rays of light extended down onto the king and the world, ending in hands, a possible symbol of the creator and giver of life aspect of Aten. During Tutankhamun's reign, a solar deity was still paramount, that of Amun-Ra, but the primary representation of solar divinity became pyramids.

The Heliopolitan solar theology did continue in the Nineteenth and Twentieth Dynasties, often known collectively as the "Ramesside Period," but Amun and the

Hermopolitan theology became much more influential, and along with it the power of Thebes.

In the aftermath of the Amarna Period, the Ramesside kings did their best to restore order throughout Egypt. Seti I (r. circa 1294–1279 BCE) restored many of the temples that were neglected by Akhenaten and erected new ones, including at Heliopolis (Dijk 2000, 295). The evidence shows that Seti I had multiple obelisks erected at Heliopolis, but the job of finishing and inscribing them was left to his son and successor, Ramesses II (r. circa 1279–1213 BCE).

Ramesses II, more commonly known as Ramesses the Great, is one of the best-known Egyptian pharaohs due to the long length of his rule. Since his reign was one of great stability and prosperity, Ramesses II was able to construct new monuments and temples throughout the land. He made additions to the Karnak and Luxor temples in Thebes, built a new mortuary temple on the west bank of Thebes, and even constructed a new city in the Delta, Per-Ramesses.

The city of Per-Ramesses, which was more than likely the Biblical Pithom, became a primary residence of the king and was located quite close to Heliopolis. An inscription on an extant obelisk from Heliopolis indicates that Ramesses finished more than one obelisk originally commissioned by Seti I. The north side of the obelisk inscriptions reads, "(Seti I), whose monuments are excellent in Heliopolis seat of eternity, like the four pillars of heaven, abiding, enduring at the forecourt of Re. The Ennead of gods is satisfied with his deeds. (May) the Son of Re, Seti-Merneptah, beloved of the gods of Heliopolis, [live] like Re."

The south side states, "(Seti I), who adorned Heliopolis for him who is therein, who purified it for Re, its lord; the lords of heaven and earth rejoice; his favor is doubled because of his deeds. May the Son of Re, Seti-Merenptah, beloved of Harakhte, live through him, like Re."

The west side reads, "(Seti I), who filled Heliopolis with obelisks, shining with rays; the house of Re is flooded with his beauty, and the gods of the Great House rejoice. May the Son of Re, Seti-Merneptah, beloved of the Ennead of gods, which is in the Great House, be given life through him."

Finally, Ramesses II includes himself on the east side's inscription: "Ramesses (II), who has made his monuments like the stars of heaven, whose works mingle with the sky, rejoicing over which Re rises in his house of millions of years. It was his majesty who beautified this monument for his father, in order to cause that his name should abide in the house of Re. May Ramesses (II)-Meriamun, beloved of Atum, lord of Heliopolis, be given life through him." (Breasted 2001, 3:229-30).

In addition to finishing the obelisks that were started by his father, Ramesses II also placed a copy of the peace treaty he concluded with Hattusilis of the Hittite Empire in the Re Temple at Heliopolis (Redford 1992, 190).

Heliopolis was certainly an important place for the first kings of the Ramesside Period, and it continued to be so throughout the Nineteenth and Twentieth Dynasties. After Ramesses II's long reign, Heliopolis was patronized by his son and successor, Merenptah (r. circa 1213–1203 BCE), and it provided a critical defensive position against invaders.

Merenptah's reign happened to coincide with the end of the Bronze Age, which in turn coincided with or resulted in the collapse of the Bronze Age Near Eastern system. The major kingdoms of the ancient Near East, which included the Egyptians, Hittites, Babylonians, and Assyrians, faced the onslaught of numerous waves of invasions by Arameans, Libyans, Sea Peoples, and others. In Egypt, a major organized invasion by Libyans and several Sea Peoples tribes took place during Merenptah's fifth year of rule.

According to a stela now known as the "Israel Stela," which was originally placed in the king's mortuary temple in Thebes, the Libyans and Sea Peoples mounted a frenzied attack on Heliopolis, but were stopped by Merenptah:

> "The All-Lord has said: 'Give the sword to my son, the upright heart, the good and kindly Merneptah, the [champion] on behalf of Memphis, the advocate of Heliopolis, who opens the towns that were closed up. Let him set free multitudes who are bound in every district, let him give offerings to the temples, let him send in incense before the god, let him cause the princes to [recover] their possessions, let him cause the poor to [re-enter] their cities.'
>
> "They say among the lords of Heliopolis regarding their son, Merneptah: 'Give to him duration like Re, let him be advocate of him who is oppressed in every country. Egypt has been assigned to him as the portion of [him who has gained it] for himself forever. His strength is its people.'" (Breasted 2001: 3:262).

In addition to the stela from Thebes, Merenptah also erected a victory column at Heliopolis to commemorate his victory, which was discovered in 1970 (Gelil et al. 1996, 137). There is no indication that the city or the solar temple suffered any serious damage, but records and evidence of building at the site are sparse for the remainder of the Nineteenth Dynasty, and it is well established that Egypt and the region were experiencing major changes at the end of the Bronze Age. New dynasties were forming throughout the Near East, and Egypt would transition into its final dynasty of the New Kingdom, the Twentieth Dynasty.

The last few kings of the Nineteenth Dynasty were inauspicious for the most part, with the dynasty ending in turmoil and confusion. When the Twentieth Dynasty came to power, it only had nominal ties to the Nineteenth Dynasty, but it attempted to draw whatever connections it could to the Ramesside kings. One way the Twentieth Dynasty kings did so was by taking the name "Ramesses," something nine of the kings did. But the most enduring and effective method was through building programs.

Ramesses III (r. 1184–1153 BCE) was as vigorous as any Twentieth Dynasty king, but he had to contend with more problems from within his country and on its borders. He successfully repelled another major invasion by the Sea Peoples and Libyans, and texts from the period show that tomb robbery and corruption were also becoming more of a problem. All these issues could have easily destabilized the fairly new dynasty, so Ramesses III embarked on an ambitious building program to get the people and the priests on his side.

A relief depicting Ramesses III

Like his predecessors in the Nineteenth Dynasty, Ramesses III built monuments in the Theban area, but he also added to the existing temple in Heliopolis. A papyrus document known as "Papyrus Harris" relates how the king expanded the temple's walls and donated numerous commodities: "I extended thy wall in the house of Re, I filled his treasury with the products of the lands of Egypt; I loaded his granaries with barley and spelt, which had begun to stand (empty) since the (former) kings. I made great designs for they [__], I cause them to rest in the shrines of thy temple; I made the regulations for the priests in the house of Re. I made him more divine than formerly, I cleansed Heliopolis for his divine ennead. I built his temples, which were gone to ruin, I fashioned their gods in their mysterious forms of gold, silver, and every costly stone, as everlasting works. . . I made for thee great monuments in the house of Re, of gritstone, which Atum shaped into great images, sculpted with toil, dragged up, and resting in their places forever and ever, in thy great, august and lovely forecourt, carved with thy divine name like the sky." (Breasted 2001, 4:142-3).

Among the more interesting sections of the papyrus are the details it discussed concerning the temple's daily operations. The Papyrus Harris is one of the most detailed accounts of the type of daily activities that went on in a temple in general, and what type and how many resources were needed to keep one running. For Heliopolis in particular, the numbers paint a picture of its extraordinary size, so much so that special storehouses were needed for large feasts and religious festivals. It reads, "I made for thee a storehouse for the 'Feast of the Appearance,' being built upon pure ground, on the land of Heliopolis, divine in workmanship. I filled it with beautiful slaves of the choicest, and clean grain by ten-thousand, in order to supply them. I made for thee a pure storehouse containing divine offerings more than were before me, since (former) kings. I equipped it with everything, it suffered no lack; in order to supply thy offerings at early morning. . . I made for thee granaries filled with grain, which had begun to fall to waste, and they became millions." (Breasted 2001, 4:144-7).

The number of people needed to operate the Heliopolis temple complex during the reign of Ramesses III was obviously immense. Nearly 13,000 male personnel and over 45,000 animals were needed, and in addition to the land that the temple complex was on and directly controlled, it had control over 103 market towns. However, despite its size and influence, the Heliopolis Temple proper only covered 170 square miles, compared to 924 square miles owned by the better known Karnak Temple (Shafter 1997, 16).

The Demise of Ancient Heliopolis

When the Twentieth Dynasty collapsed and Egypt once more entered the Third Intermediate Period, the situation remained somewhat unchanged for Heliopolis. Although central rule had collapsed in the Third Intermediate Period as it had in the previous two periods of that type, powerful Libyan-descended dynasties formed in the Delta. These dynasties rarely battled each other and were quite content to divide up the country among themselves.

As they were dividing Egypt, some also made attempts to appear as legitimate Egyptian rulers by conducting building programs and by patronizing Egyptian deities and religious institutions. Siamun (r. 978–959 BCE), the fourth king of the Twenty-First Dynasty, which primarily ruled from the Delta city of Tanis, added a short inscription to one of Thutmose III's obelisks at Heliopolis (Kitchen 1995, 279). Later kings of the Third Intermediate and Late Period would be much more generous toward Heliopolis, viewing patronage of the city and the solar religion as a major boost to their rule over Egypt.

The Twenty-Second Dynasty proved to be the most stable and powerful Third Intermediate Period dynasty, although its rule over all of Egypt was tenuous, and by the end of the dynasty it shared the land with the Twenty-Third Dynasty. The first five kings of the Twenty-Second Dynasty were quite powerful though, and they tightly controlled the region around Heliopolis (Kitchen 1995, 347).

The reputation of Heliopolis, and the site was considered so important that Shoshenq I (r. 945–925 BCE), the first king of the Twenty-Second Dynasty, added monuments to the city. Acknowledging Heliopolis' longstanding importance for the Egyptian religion, Shoshenq I even referred to Thebes as the "Southern Heliopolis." An inscription from a relief at Karnak reads, "Utterance of Amun-Re…'My heart is very glad, when I see thy victories, my son, Meriamun-Sheshonk, my beloved, who camest forth from me, in order to be my champion. I have seen the excellence of thy plans; which thou hast executed, the ____ of my temple, my hear [inclines]. Thou hast begun to make monuments in Southern Heliopolis, Northern Heliopolis, and every city.'" (Breasted 2001, 4:356) .

The inscription was part of a much larger text that detailed Shoshenq I's more famous military campaign into Israel. According to that text, the Egyptian king led a plundering campaign through several Israelite cities before returning to Egypt with plenty of prizes (Kitchen 1995, 432–47). After returning to Egypt, Shoshenq I then distributed the booty to several cities, but apparently Thebes and Heliopolis were the major recipients.

Shoshenq I's successor, Osorokon I (r. 924–889 BCE), left inscriptions at Karnak, but he also bestowed gifts and furniture to the many temples of Heliopolis (Kitchen 1995, 303). When the archaeological remains of Heliopolis are considered along with the textual references mentioned here, it is reasonable to believe that the temple complex of Heliopolis was comparable to that of Karnak. Amun may have become the most important god in the New Kingdom, but in the Third Intermediate Period, the solar cult of Heliopolis was nearly, if not equally, as important to most kings. Nonetheless, the evidence indicates that building activity at Heliopolis appears to have come to a halt for more than 150 years after Osorkon I's rule. The political order of Egypt devolved into Libyan-descended dynasties that, although not warring among each other, made no attempts to unify the land.

The desire to unify Egypt under one king would come from the south. in Nubia. The Nubians had been connected to Egypt through trade and at times as a colony since the Old Kingdom, but in the 1st millennium BCE the Nubians were powerful enough to assert themselves over their former masters. A Nubian king named Piye, or Piankhy, led a major military campaign north from the Nubian city of Napata, defeating Libyan leaders until he finally took Heliopolis and the Delta. After his military victory in 728 BCE, the surviving Libyan chieftains came to Piye in obeisance, which was recorded in a hieroglyphic inscription on a stela known as "Piye's Victory Stela."

Heliopolis played a role in the victory, both strategically and spiritually. Part of the stela reads:

> "At dawn of the next day his majesty proceeded to the East. An offering was made to Atum in Kheraha, the Ennead in Per-Pesdjet, and the cavern of the gods in it, consisting of oxen, shorthorns, and fowl, that they might give life-prosperity-health to the King of Upper and Lower

Egypt, Piye ever living.

> "His majesty proceeded to On over that mountain of Kheraha on the road of Sep to Kheraha. His majesty went to the camp on the west of Iti. His purification wad done: he was cleansed in the pool of Kebeh; his face was bathed in the river of Nun, in which Re bathes his face. He proceeded to the High Sand in On. . . Entering the temple of Atum. Worshipping the image of his father Atum-Khepri, Great one of On." (Lichtheim 1980, 3:76-77).

When he entered the solar temple in Heliopolis, Piye donated plenty of gifts and offerings: "Going in procession to the temple of Re. Entering the temple with adorations. The chief lector-priest's praising god and repulsing the rebels from the king. Performing the ritual of the robing room; putting on the *sdb*-garment; cleansing him with incense and cold water; presenting him the garlands of the Pyramidion House; bringing him the amulets." (Lichtheim 1980, 3:77). Piye then went to the Delta city of Arthribis to accept the formal surrender of his enemies before returning to Nubia.

Egypt's last gasp of greatness came during the Twenty-Sixth Dynasty, when a family of kings from the Delta city of Sais reintroduced many elements of earlier Egyptian art and literature and attempted to establish some of the kingdom's old imperial glory. The first king of the dynasty (often called the Saite Dynasty after their capital city), Psamtek I (r. circa 664–610 BCE), was responsible for expelling the Nubians and Assyrians and for establishing many of the hallmarks of Late Period culture. Most of Psamtek I's major building projects were in the areas of Memphis and Thebes, but there is evidence that he built throughout the Delta. Building fragments recovered from Alexandria show that he built a temple for Atum and the Heliopolitan Ennead at Sais (Arnold 1999, 71).

Though there is reason to believe that he also built in Heliopolis, there is no direct evidence that Psamtek I built anything significant in Heliopolis. However, one of his successors certainly did. Psamtek II (r. 595–589 BCE) is best known for leading a military campaign into Nubia and for involving Egypt in the affairs of the Kingdom of Israel and the Neo-Babylonian Empire. Although he was not particularly known for being a builder, Psamtek II is credited with erecting two obelisks measuring more than 70 feet at Heliopolis (Arnold 1999, 76). Like many of Egypt's obelisks, these were taken away by the Romans, but the geographer Strabo offered a description of them, a layout of the sun temple in Heliopolis, and the layout of many Egyptian temples in general.

Strabo wrote:

> "Two of these, which were not completely spoiled, were brought to Rome, but others are either sill there or at Thebes, the present Diospolis – some still standing, thoroughly eaten by the fire, and others lying on the ground.
>
> "The plan of the construction of the temples is as follows: at the entrance into the sacred precinct there is a floor paved with stones, with a breadth of about a plethrum, or less, and a length either three or four times as great, or in some cases more; and this is called the dromus, as Callimachus states: "This the dromus, sacred to Anubis." Throughout its whole length are stone sphinxes placed in order on each of its two sides, at a distance form one another of twenty cubits or a little more, so that one row of the sphinxes is on the right and one row on the left. And after the sphinxes one comes to a large propylum, and then, as one proceeds, another, and then another; but there is no prescribed number either of propyla or of sphinxes…" (Strabo, *Geography*, XVII, 1 27-28).

Heliopolis was certainly still an impressive and important place in Egypt in the 6th century BCE, but its days were numbered. The changes in culture and geopolitics meant that it would eventually be overlooked in favor of other cities, but for the remainder of the Twenty-Sixth Dynasty and through the Thirtieth Dynasty, it appears that Heliopolis still retained most of its solar glory. The Twenty-Sixth Dynasty's King Apries (r. 589–570 BCE) commissioned two quartzite sphinxes at Heliopolis (Arnold 1999, 171), and the first king of the Thirtieth Dynasty, Nectanebo I (r. 379–361 BCE) added to the Heliopolitan Temple in Sais (Arnold 1999, 171). But as much as Heliopolis was revered by both Egyptians and Greeks, it eventually became the victim of a trend in the region that could not be reversed.

The diminishing influence of Egypt and the growing power of the Greek city-states could not be denied by the 6th century BCE. Already by the 7th century BCE, Greeks had been immigrating to Egypt at the invitation of the Saite kings. The Greeks lived and worked in Egypt as merchants and mercenaries and established a colony in Naucratis and a neighborhood in Memphis. Outside of Egypt, the Greeks were the only people who effectively opposed the Achaemenid Persian Empire, and it was Athenians who supported Egyptian rebellions against the Persian Thirty-First Dynasty in Egypt. The Greeks were clearly the dominant force in the region by the 4th century, but as noted earlier, they acknowledged that Heliopolis was once a place of great learning. According to Strabo, merchants and mercenaries were not the only Greeks who spent considerable time in Egypt; philosophers such as Plato visited Heliopolis to soak up some of the ancient city's wisdom. Strabo wrote, "In Heliupolis I also saw large houses in which the priests lived; for it is said that his place in particular was in ancient times a settlement of priests who studied philosophy and astronomy; but both this organisation and its pursuits have now disappeared. At Heliupolis, in fact, no one was pointed out to me as presiding over such pursuits, but only those who performed the sacrifices and explained to strangers what pertained to the sacred rites. When Aelius Gallus the praefect sailed up into Aegypt, he was accompanied by a certain man from Alexandria, Chaeremon by name, who pretended to some knowledge of this kind, but was generally ridiculed as a boaster and ignoramus. However, at Heliupolis the houses of the priests and schools of Plato and Eudoxus were point out to us; for Eudoxus went up to that place with Plato, and they both passed thirteen years with the priests, as is stated by some writers." (Strabo *Geography*, XVII, I, 27).

Although Plato was known to have visited Egypt later in his life, it seems unlikely that he learned the Egyptian language well enough to study under the priests at Heliopolis. With that said, the passage does demonstrate that Heliopolis was still held in high regard by non-Egyptians at the time.

When Alexander the Great conquered Egypt in 332 BCE, it began a period of Greek rule. Alexander himself toured parts of Egypt, visiting the Siwa Oasis and the capital of Memphis. According to the 2nd century CE Greek historian Arrian, Alexander entered Egypt in the Delta and traveled through Heliopolis before entering the capital: "Alexander garrisoned at Pelusium and, after giving orders to the fleet to proceed up the Nile to Memphis, set out southward along the east bank of the river, and, crossing the desert, arrived at Heliopolis. All the country along his route he secured without any native opposition. From Heliopolis he crossed the river to Memphis, where, among the other gods, he offered a special sacrifice to Apis and held Games with both athletic and literary contests." (Arrian, *The Campaigns of Alexander,* Book III, 1).

The account gives no other details about Heliopolis other than that it was a waypoint for the Macedonian conqueror, but since it was mentioned, it likely still held some significance for the Greeks at the time, even if its spiritual significance was greatly diminished. After all, Heliopolis had an oracle that Alexander could have consulted, but he bypassed it in favor of the oracle in the Siwa Oasis in the Sahara Desert.

Alexander's conquest represented the beginning of the final phase in Heliopolis' long history. The Ptolemaic Dynasty was officially founded in 305 BCE by Ptolemy I, one of Alexander's trusted generals, after Alexander's death, and the Ptolemies dedicated most of their resources to the construction of their very Greek city, Alexandria. Although the Ptolemies continued to patronize most of the native Egyptian cults and the temples stayed open, there is no doubt that large parts of the country became backwaters compared to Alexandria.

That said, there is evidence that early Ptolemaic rulers continued to patronize Heliopolis. A statue of Ptolemy II (r. 284–246 BCE), the second Ptolemaic king and his wife Arsinoe II, discovered in Rome is believed to have originally stood in Heliopolis (Arnold 1999, 158), but little more can be connected to the city after him. The later Ptolemaic kings were more interested in finances, fighting the Seleucid Dynasty, and cozying up to Rome than they were in building at Heliopolis.

When the Romans incorporated Egypt into their empire in 30 BCE, Heliopolis' greatness had long since passed, and it had apparently become deserted. When Strabo visited Egypt during the reign of Augustus, he noted that Heliopolis had been vacant for some time: "Here are both the city Bubastus and the Bubastite Nome; and above it is the Heliopolite Nome. In this Nome is Heliupolis, which is situated upon a noteworthy mound; it contains the temple of Helios, and the ox Mneuïs, which is kept in a kind of sanctuary and is regarded among the inhabitants as god, as is Apis in Memphis. In front of the mound are lakes, which receive the overflow from the neighboring canal. The city is now entirely deserted; it contains the ancient temple constructed in the Aegyptian manner." (Strabo *Geography*, XVII, I, 27).

Not surprisingly, the Romans found the obelisks of Heliopolis eclectically interesting, so they began to transport them to Rome, marking the beginning of the city's dismantling. The rise of Christianity and then Islam ensured that the sun temple would never again be patronized, and Egypt's growing population meant that its pieces would all be systematically taken down.

Long after Egyptian civilization collapsed and knowledge of the enigmatic hieroglyphic script was lost in the sands, memories of the ancient Egyptian culture remained. The Greek historians, the Biblical narratives, and the towering presence of the pyramids and temples of Egypt helped keep alive the memory of pharaonic culture. Following Napoleon's conquest of Egypt in the late 1700s, a wave of French scholars and explorers, known as *savants*, fanned out across Egypt in order to uncover its ancient mysteries. The ruins of Heliopolis, though, were nearly overlooked in the first rush of archaeological inquiry. Besides the ravages of age, Heliopolis suffered from being built on a high water table with plenty of mud, surrounded by immense urban development (Nuzzolo and Krejčí 2017, 358), and over the centuries, local peasant farmers continually used blocks from the city and temple complex for their own building structures and for fertilizer. The creation of Cairo in the Middle Ages and its subsequent boom in population also contributed to the decline of Heliopolis, which is today a suburb of Cairo.

Fortunately, even as these things contributed to the near total demise of ancient Heliopolis, one giant obelisk that remained at the site suggested to the French explorers that it was once a significant city. The French conducted the first scientific surveys of Heliopolis in the late 1700s and early 1800s, but even when Egyptology became a legitimate, independent discipline by the mid-19th century, the site garnered little interest from professionals. Due to the reasons mentioned above, excavating Heliopolis was extremely difficult, so archaeologists bypassed it in favor of better-known sites, which proved to be lower hanging fruit.

Fortunately, as knowledge of the ancient Egyptian language grew, so too did the realization that Heliopolis was one of ancient Egypt's most important religious sites. The Italian archeologist Ernesto Schiaparelli was the first scholar to conduct a major excavation at Heliopolis. From

1903-1904, Schiaparelli did a preliminary excavation of Heliopolis, which was followed by a much more extensive excavation and mapping of the sitc by Englishman Flinders Petrie in 1912. Petrie surveyed the site and determined its original size. He also did some digging, uncovering enough to determine that the city was as important as the ancient texts described it (Nuzzolo and Krejčí 2017, 358).

After Petrie, archaeological interest in Heliopolis waned once more until the 1990s, when German Dietrich Raue and others applied new technology and methods to uncovering some of the sun city's secrets (Gelil et al. 1996). Given what is already known about Heliopolis and what the Egyptians themselves wrote about their vital religious site, it's clear that plenty of work remains to be done there.

Online Resources

Other Egyptian history titles by Charles River Editors

Other titles about Heliopolis on Amazon

Further Reading

Arrian. 1971. *The Campaigns of Alexander*. Translated by Aubrey de Sélincourt. London: Penguin Books.

Arnold, Dieter. 1999. *Temples of the Last Pharaohs*.

Oxford: Oxford University Press.

Assman, Jan. 2001. *The Search for God in Ancient Egypt*. Translated by David Lorton. Ithaca, New York: Cornell University Press.

Breasted, James Henry, ed. and trans. 2001. *Ancient Records of Egypt.* 4 Vols. Champaign, Illinois: University of Illinois Press.

Bryan, Betsy. "The 18th Dynasty before the Amarna Period." In *The Oxford History of Ancient Egypt*, edited by Ian Shaw, 218–271. Oxford: Oxford University Press.

Callender, Gae. 2000. "The Middle Kingdom Renaissance (c. 2055-1650 BC)." In *The Oxford History of Ancient Egypt*, edited by Ian Shaw, 148–183. Oxford: Oxford University Press.

Dijk, Jacobus van. 2000. "The Amarna Period and the Later New Kingdom." In *The Oxford History of Ancient Egypt*, edited by Ian Shaw, 272–313. Oxford: Oxford University Press.

Diodorus Siculus. 2004. *The Library of History.* Translated by C.H. Oldfather. Cambridge, Massachusetts: Harvard University Press.

Faulkner, Richard O. *The Ancient Egyptian Pyramid Texts.* Stilwell, Kansas: Digireads.com Publishing, 2007.

———. 1999. *A Dictionary of Middle Egyptian*. Oxford: Griffith Institute.

Gelil, Mohammed Abd el, Mohammed Shaker, and Dietrich Raue. 1996. "Recent Excavations at Heliopolis." *Orientalia* 65: 136-146.

Grajetzki, Wolfram. 2009. *The Middle Kingdom of Ancient Egypt*. London: Duckworth.

Haeny, Gerhard. 1997. "New Kingdom 'Mortuary Temples' and 'Mansions of Millions of Years." In *Temples of Ancient Egypt*, edited by Byron E. Shaffer, 86–126. Ithaca, New York: Cornell University Press.

Herodotus. 2003. *The Histories*. Translated by Aubrey de Sélincourt. London: Penguin Books.

Hornung, Erik. 1996. *Conceptions of God in Ancient Egypt: The One an the Many*. Translated by John Baines. Ithaca, New York: Cornell University Press.

Kemp, Barry J. 1991. *Ancient Egypt: Anatomy of a Civilization*. London: Routledge.

Kitchen, Kenneth A. *The Third Intermediate Period in Egypt: (1100 to 650 BC)*. 2nd ed.

Warminster, United Kingdom: Aris and Phillips, 1995.

Krebsbach, Jared. 2014. "Herodotus, Diodorus, and

Manetho: An Examination of the Influence of Egyptian Historiography on the Classical Historians." *New England Classical Journal* 41: 88–111.

Lichtheim, Miriam, ed. 1976–2006. *Ancient Egyptian Literature*. 3 vols. Los Angeles: University of California Press.

Malek, Jaromir. 2000. "The Old Kingdom (c. 2686-2125 BC)." In *The Oxford History of Ancient Egypt*, edited by Ian Shaw, 89-117. Oxford: Oxford University Press.

Manetho. 2004. *Aegyptiaca.* Translated by W. G. Waddell. Cambridge, Massachusetts: Harvard University Press.

Nuzzolo, Massimiliano, and Jaromír Krejčí. 2017. "Heliopolis and the Solar Cult in the Third Millennium BC." *Ägypten und Levante* 27: 357–380.

Redford, Donald B. 1992. *Egypt, Canaan, and Israel in Ancient Times*. Princeton, New Jersey: Princeton University Press.

Robins, Gay. 2000. *The Art of Ancient Egypt*. Cambridge, Massachusetts: Harvard University Press.

Shaw, Ian and Paul Nicholson. 1995. *The Dictionary of Ancient Egypt*. New York: Harry N. Abrams.

Shafer, Byron. 1997. "Temples, Priests, and Rituals: An

Overview." In *Temples of Ancient Egypt*, edited by Byron E. Shaffer, 1–30. Ithaca, New York: Cornell University Press.

Strabo. 2001. *Geography*. Translated by Horace Leonard Jones. Cambridge, Massachusetts: Harvard University Press.

Tobin, Vincent Arieh. 2002. "Creation Myths." In *The Ancient Gods Speak: A Guide to Egyptian Religion*, edited by Donald B. Redford, 246–251. Oxford: Oxford University Press, 2002

Wilkinson, Richard H. 2003. *The Complete Gods and Goddesses of Ancient Egypt.* London: Thames and Hudson.

Free Books by Charles River Editors

We have brand new titles available for free most days of the week. To see which of our titles are currently free, click on this link.

Discounted Books by Charles River Editors

We have titles at a discount price of just 99 cents everyday. To see which of our titles are currently 99 cents, click on this link.

Printed in Great Britain
by Amazon

45811311R00056